The Story of
Helen Keller

by Rachel A. Koestler-Grack

CHELSEA CLUBHOUSE

An Imprint of Chelsea House Publishers

A Haights Cross Communications Company

Philadelphia

Chelsea Clubhouse books are published by Chelsea House Publishers, a subsidiary of Haights Cross Communications.

A Haights Cross Communications ✦ Company

The Chelsea House World Wide Web address is www.chelseahouse.com

Printed and bound in the United States of America.

9 8 7 6 5 4 3 2 1

Library of Congress Cataloging-in-Publication Data
Koestler-Grack, Rachel A., 1973–
  The story of Helen Keller / by Rachel A. Koestler-Grack.
     p. cm. — (Breakthrough biographies)
Summary: Introduces Helen Keller and tells of her childhood struggles with deafness and blindness which led her to a successful career as a public speaker, writer, and champion of rights for the disabled.
Includes bibliographical references and index.
  ISBN 0-7910-7315-7
1. Keller, Helen, 1880–1968—Juvenile literature. 2. Blind-deaf women—United States—Biography—Juvenile literature.
3. Blind-deaf—United States—Biography—Juvenile literature. 4. Sullivan, Annie, 1866–1936—Juvenile literature.
[1. Keller, Helen, 1880–1968. 2. Blind. 3. Deaf. 4. People with disabilities. 5. Women—Biography. 6. Sullivan, Annie, 1866–1936.]
I. Title. II. Series.
HV1624.K4K64 2004
362.4'1'092—dc21   2003000366

Selected Sources

Harrity, Richard and Ralph G. Martin. *The Three Lives of Helen Keller*. Garden City, NY: Doubleday & Co., 1962.

Hermann, Dorothy. *Helen Keller: A Life*. New York: Alfred A. Knopf, 1998.

Keller, Helen. *The Story of My Life*. New York: Penguin Putnam, reprinted 2002.

Keller, Helen. *The World I Live In*. New York: The Century Co., 1908.

Lash, Joseph. *Helen and Teacher: The Story of Helen Keller and Anne Sullivan Macy*. New York: Delacorte Press, 1980.

Editorial Credits

Colleen Sexton and Laura Hamilton Waxman, editors; Takeshi Takahashi, designer;
Mary Englar, photo researcher; Jennifer Krassy Peiler, layout

Content Reviewer

Jan Seymour-Ford, Research Librarian, Perkins School for the Blind, Watertown, Massachusetts

Photo Credits

©Bettmann/CORBIS: cover, 5, 12, 22, 29 (Nellie Bly); ©Bradley Smith/CORBIS: title page, 27 (top); American Foundation for the Blind, Helen Keller Archives: 4, 8, 17, 21 (left), 23, 24; Helen Keller Birthplace Foundation: 6; ©Walter Sanders/Time Life Pictures/Getty Images: 7; ©Corbis: 9; Perkins School for the Blind: 10, 11, 15 (top), 16, 21 (right), 25, 27 (bottom); North Wind Picture Archives: 13; Library of Congress: 14, 18, 19, 20; ©Craig Hammell/CORBIS: 15 (bottom); ©Hulton/Archive by Getty Images: 26; AP/Wide World: 29 (Rachel Carson, Annie Oakley, Georgia O'Keefe, Eleanor Roosevelt); Rick Apitz: back cover

Table of Contents

A Shining Example

Helen Keller was nervous and scared. At age 33, she was about to give her first public speech to an audience. But she couldn't see or hear the large crowd that eagerly awaited her lecture. Helen was blind and deaf. At that moment, "terror invaded my flesh, my mind froze, my heart stopped beating," Helen later remembered. Still, she wanted to talk about her life and help people understand her **disability**. So she gathered up her courage and stepped onto the stage.

The First Appearance on the Lecture Platform of

HELEN KELLER

And her Teacher Mrs. Macy (Anne M. Sullivan)

SUBJECT

"The Heart and the Hand," or the Right Use of our Senses

Under the exclusive Management of
J. B. POND LYCEUM BUREAU
Metropolitan Life Building
New York City

This poster announced Helen Keller's first public lecture, which she titled "The Heart and the Hand, or the Right Use of Our Senses."

Helen's first lecture in 1913 led to a 48-year career of giving speeches to audiences throughout the world.

Helen gave her lecture with her teacher and friend, Annie Sullivan, at her side. Speaking was difficult for Helen. If the crowd had trouble understanding her, Annie carefully repeated Helen's words. Finally, Helen's first lecture came to an end. She left the stage in tears, certain that she had done terribly. But she was wrong. The audience rose to its feet, clapping and cheering.

> *"Blind people are just like seeing people in the dark. The loss of sight does not impair the qualities of mind and heart."*
> —Helen Keller

Again and again, Helen Keller faced the challenge of being both deaf and blind. She devoted her life to proving that people with disabilities can lead normal, productive lives. Her courage and determination made her a shining example for people all over the world.

Suddenly Dark

Helen was born a healthy seeing-and-hearing baby on June 27, 1880, in Tuscumbia, Alabama. She was the first child of Kate and Arthur Keller. Helen later wrote, "The beginning of my life was simple and much like every other little life."

Helen was a bright child with golden hair and blue eyes. By the time she was 6 months old, she could say "How d'ye" and "tea, tea, tea." Helen also knew the meaning of the word "water." When she was thirsty, she asked for "wah-wah." On her first birthday, Helen took her first steps.

One day in February 1882, Helen suddenly became ill with a high fever. She suffered from a bad headache and a stiff neck. Helen's doctor called her illness a "brain fever," a name commonly given to any unknown illness at that time. Both the doctor and Helen's family feared she might die. But after several days, the fever broke and Helen's temperature returned to normal. The Kellers were relieved.

Helen grew up at Ivy Green, her family's home on a large farm in Tuscumbia, Alabama. Helen liked to play with the farm's horses and dogs. One of her chores was feeding the chickens.

Helen's parents were Arthur and Kate Keller. Smart and well read, Kate was also an energetic housekeeper and loving mother. Arthur ran the local newspaper and was known as a good host, who enjoyed entertaining guests at Ivy Green.

But soon Kate and Arthur noticed that something was terribly wrong with their 19-month-old daughter. When Kate called out to Helen, she didn't respond. Even when Kate shouted, Helen didn't move. Helen's parents also noticed that she didn't look at them. She seemed to stare blankly. Arthur waved his hand in front of Helen's face. She didn't blink. Arthur and Kate realized their daughter could no longer see or hear.

Because Helen could not hear people speak, she could not learn to talk as other children do. She tried to **communicate** in other ways. "A shake of the head meant 'No' and a nod 'Yes,' a pull meant 'Come' and a push 'Go,'" Helen later explained.

Helen soon used other made-up signals. When she wanted her father, she pretended to put on eyeglasses. She stroked her cheek or pulled her hair back when she wanted her mother. In time, Helen realized that her family didn't use signals to talk to each other. Helen later wrote, "I do not remember when I first realized that I was different from other people; but . . . I had noticed that my mother and my friends did not use signs as I did when they wanted anything done, but talked with their mouths."

As she grew older, Helen became angry that she couldn't communicate with others. She broke dishes and lamps. She also figured out how to use a key and one day locked her mother in the pantry on purpose.

> *"I was too young to realize what had happened. When I awoke and found that all was dark and still, I suppose I thought it was night, and I must have wondered why day was so long coming."*
>
> —Helen Keller

Helen tried to move her lips, but she could not form words. She later wrote, "This made me so angry at times that I kicked and screamed until I was exhausted." Helen wanted people to understand her. As she grew older, she became more and more **frustrated**. She often threw temper tantrums. She bit, hit, and pinched other people when she became angry or did not get her way. Helen later admitted she was a "wild, destructive little animal." She was trapped in her own silent, dark world.

People with Disabilities in Helen's Time

When Helen was growing up in the 1800s, people with disabilities faced great **prejudice**. Some families saw their disabled children as a burden and never thought to give them an education. Other parents protected children with disabilities by hiding them. They refused to take their children to public places where they would be stared at, pitied, pushed aside, or feared. Many store and restaurant owners did not allow people with disabilities into their businesses. They worried that one of their customers might not want to shop or eat near a disabled person.

Employers also treated people with disabilities unfairly. Many people with disabilities can work just as well as someone who is not disabled. But business owners didn't want to hire them. They didn't believe a person in a wheelchair or a person who was blind or deaf could do proper work. Like many people, employers thought those with disabilities could not lead productive lives.

Today, people with disabilities are valued members of society who live full lives. Although they still deal with prejudice, their rights are now protected under the law. The Americans with Disabilities Act passed in 1990 says that employers, businesses, and the government must treat people with disabilities fairly.

Taken in about 1900, this photograph shows students playing outside Overbrook School for the Blind in Philadelphia. By this time, many blind children were attending special schools. Today, the majority of children who are blind go to regular schools.

A Teacher

Arthur and Kate wanted to help Helen. When their daughter was 6 years old, Arthur wrote a letter to the Perkins Institution for the Blind in Boston, Massachusetts. He wanted to find a teacher for Helen.

The director of the institute suggested a former student named Anne Mansfield Sullivan to be Helen's teacher. As a child, Annie had a serious eye disease that left her almost blind. After having surgery on her eyes, she could see again.

But her earlier blindness would help her understand some of Helen's frustrations. Twenty-one-year-old Annie came to live with the Kellers on March 3, 1887. Helen later called that date the most important day in all her life.

Opened in Boston in 1832, Perkins Institution for the Blind was the first school for the blind in the United States. Helen's teacher, Annie Sullivan, graduated from the school in 1886. Helen would also spend time studying at Perkins.

Annie Sullivan became Helen's teacher in 1887 and spent the rest of her life as Helen's aid and companion. In 1905, Annie married a writer named John Macy, but the marriage lasted only nine years.

Annie began by teaching Helen words. One day Annie placed a doll in Helen's hands. As Helen held onto her doll with one hand, Annie pressed the letters D-O-L-L into the palm of the girl's other hand. Annie spelled with a manual alphabet used by people who are deaf. Each letter in this type of alphabet had a different hand sign. Normally, a person who is deaf would look at the hand signs to understand them. Because Helen also couldn't see, Annie had to make sure Helen could feel the hand signs.

Annie spelled the word "doll" again and again into Helen's palm. Finally, Helen picked up Annie's hand and pressed the letters D-O-L-L into her teacher's palm. "I did not know that I was spelling a word or that words even existed. I was simply making my fingers go in monkey-like imitation," Helen later remembered. Soon Helen learned other words, such as "cake," "hat," and "walk." But Helen thought it was just a game. She didn't understand that the words had meaning.

It was at this water pump at Ivy Green that Helen realized the hand signs Annie made were words. "A new light came into her face," Annie later remembered.

One day in April, Annie and Helen stopped at a water pump. Annie began to pump water out of the spout. She took one of Helen's hands and placed it underneath the cool water. In Helen's other hand, Annie spelled out W-A-T-E-R. She spelled it over and over again. "Suddenly.... the mystery of language was revealed to me," Helen later recalled. "I knew that W-A-T-E-R meant the wonderful cool something that was flowing over my hand."

That day, Helen learned many new words, including "mother," "father," and "sister." And she learned that Annie was "Teacher." Helen later wrote, "It would have been difficult to find a happier child than I was . . . at the close of that eventful day. For the first time [I] longed for a new day to come."

The Manual Alphabet and Sign Language

In 1816, educator Thomas Hopkins Gallaudet returned to the United States from Europe. During a visit to France, he had learned to use sign language to communicate with the deaf. Eager to teach this system of hand **gestures**, he founded a school for the deaf in 1817. From this early use, American Sign Language (ASL) developed. Today in the United States, ASL is the most common way for people who are deaf to communicate.

ASL uses signs for ideas, rather than words. A single hand or arm gesture can communicate a concept, such as how the weather is. Within ASL, a manual alphabet—also called a finger alphabet—is used to spell out specific words, such as a name. The manual alphabet has 26 hand signs, one for each letter of the alphabet. A deaf and blind person like Helen Keller could spell out words by feeling these signs as they were made into her hand.

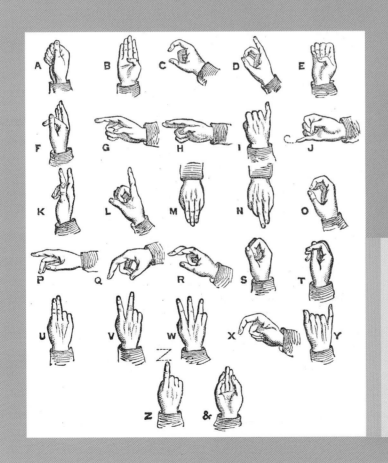

The manual alphabet has a hand sign for each letter of the alphabet. Many people who are deaf communicate by using a combination of the manual alphabet and American Sign Language.

Learning to Speak

During the spring of 1887, Helen learned hundreds of words. With Annie as her guide, Helen made great new discoveries, such as how plants grow and how birds build their nests.

"As my knowledge of things grew I felt more and more the delight of the world I was in," she later described.

Annie decided it was time to teach Helen to read. They started with special books from the Perkins Institution that had pages printed in raised letters. Before long, Helen could read the small books from start to finish. Later, Helen

In this photograph, Annie shows how she signs words into Helen's hand. After Helen learned the manual alphabet, she later remembered, "I did nothing but explore with my hands and learn the name of every object that I touched."

By 1888, Helen had learned to read Braille. Here, she reads with her left hand and signs the words with her right hand.

learned to read **Braille**. Each letter in this reading system is made up of a combination of raised dots. Helen ran her fingers over the dots to read the letters and words. Soon Helen was reading entire books in Braille.

Annie also taught Helen to write. Helen placed her paper on a special board that had grooves where lines would be. As she wrote, she followed a groove in order to write in a straight line. It was hard work. Helen ended many of her first letters to friends and relatives with the words "I am tired."

"More than at any other time, when I hold a beloved book in my hand my limitations fall from me, my spirit is free."
—Helen Keller

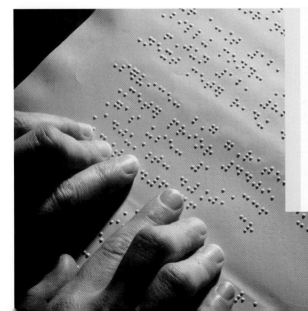

People who are blind read by feeling a code of raised dots with their hands. Frenchman Louis Braille developed this reading system in the 1820s. In addition to the alphabet, the Braille system includes punctuation marks and numbers. Louis Braille also developed a code for music.

When she was 9 years old, Helen decided she wanted to learn to speak with her voice. Her teacher was Sarah Fuller, the principal at a school for the deaf. Miss Fuller taught Helen to feel sounds with her fingers. Helen learned to gently place her hand on Miss Fuller's face. Then Helen felt her teacher's mouth and tongue as she spoke. She also felt the **vibrations** in Miss Fuller's throat. In one hour, Helen learned to speak six letters—M, P, A, S, T, and I. After 10 lessons, Helen could speak a complete sentence. But talking out loud was difficult for Helen. She never learned to speak as clearly as she wanted. Still, she later wrote, "Even when the speech is not beautiful there is a fountain of joy in uttering words."

As she was learning to speak, Helen also learned to read lips. Here, Helen feels how the words are formed by Annie's mouth as she speaks.

In this portrait, Helen is 13 years old. Many early photographs show only the right side of Helen's face to hide her left eye, which was damaged. Helen later had both eyes replaced with real-looking glass eyes.

By age 13, Helen had become famous. Newspapers featured articles about her disabilities and her accomplishments. Reporters called Helen "the wonder girl" and "a miracle." Not long ago, she had been locked in silence and darkness. Now she inspired people around the world.

> *"True, I cannot see the stars scattered like gold-dust in the heavens, but other stars just as bright shine in my soul."*
> —Helen Keller

Telling Her Story

When Helen was 16 years old, she chose a new challenge. She wanted to go to a college where the students could see and hear. She chose Radcliffe College, a school in Massachusetts for women. Helen needed to take several difficult tests to attend Radcliffe. She studied and studied until she was able to pass them. Helen finally started college in the fall of 1900, at age 20. She was the first person with her disabilities to attend a college or university.

Helen wanted to be treated like the other students. She attended regular classes and typed her papers on a typewriter. Annie was almost always at Helen's side, signing class lectures into her hand. Helen received excellent grades. But fitting in with the other students proved more difficult. Helen's fame made some

At Radcliffe College, Annie was at Helen's side to help her through her studies. Helen also had the company of her dog, Phiz, given to her by a group of fellow students.

In her writings, Helen shared how she experienced the world as a woman who was blind and deaf.

classmates shy away from her. Others thought communicating with her was too hard. Only a few friends learned the manual alphabet so they could talk with Helen directly.

In one of her classes, Helen wrote an **essay** about her life. The essay came to the attention of the editor of a popular magazine called *Ladies' Home Journal*. The editor was impressed and asked Helen to write a series of articles about herself for the magazine. In these short pieces, Helen told readers about her frustrations and her joys.

"I seldom think of my limitations, and they never make me sad. Perhaps there is just a touch of yearning at times; but it is vague, like a breeze among flowers."
—Helen Keller

In the spring of 1903, Helen published the articles in a book titled *The Story of My Life*. At age 22, Helen had become an author. Her book was a great success. Reviewers praised Helen's writing style. And readers were eager to learn about the life of someone who was deaf and blind.

When Helen graduated from Radcliffe College in 1904, she was nervous about what she would do next and how she would support herself.

Helen graduated from Radcliffe with honors a year later, in 1904. With Annie's help, Helen continued to write. In 1908, she published a second successful book about her life, *The World I Live In*. People were curious about Helen. She decided to give lectures about her challenges to encourage other people who faced difficulties in their lives. She also wanted people to better understand those who were deaf or blind.

Helen and Annie began giving lectures around the United States. Annie spoke first and explained how she had taught Helen to read and write. They then demonstrated the manual alphabet. Finally, Helen spoke to the crowd and answered their questions. Later, she remembered that "the audience was always patient. Whether they understood me or not, they showered me with good wishes and flowers and encouragement."

In 1918, Helen found another way to share her story. She and Annie traveled to Los Angeles, where Helen starred in a movie about her life called *Deliverance*. On camera, Helen read Braille and acted out her everyday activities. She typed on her Braille typewriter and played a trumpet. She even rode a horse. When the movie opened, the *New York Times* called it "one of the triumphs of the motion picture." Helen and Annie were disappointed, however, when the movie drew only small audiences.

> *"What a strange life I lead—a kind of Cinderella-life—half glitter in crystal shoes, half mice and cinders! But it is a wonderful life all the same."*
> —Helen Keller

A poster (right) advertised the opening of *Deliverance*, a film about Helen's life. Helen starred in the movie, which also featured an appearance by her brother Philp and her mother (above).

THE 8th Wonder of the World
Helen Keller
IN THE PHOTO-PLAY BEAUTIFUL
"DELIVERANCE"

TOGETHER WITH HER LIFE LONG FRIEND, COMPANION and BELOVED INSTRUCTOR
ANNE SULLIVAN (MACY)
BOTH APPEARING PERSONALLY IN THIS MOST INTERESTING and INCOMPARABLE OF PHOTO-PLAYS

DIRECT FROM HER TRIUMPHANT TOUR OF AMERICA'S BEST THEATRES

TREMONT TEMPLE | Commencing Mon. Eve JULY 19

In 1931, Helen attended a luncheon at the White House for the World Conference on Work for the Blind. Standing in the front row and wearing a light-colored coat, Helen posed with other people at the conference.

In 1924, Helen decided to take a more direct role in helping people with disabilities. She became a member of a new organization called the American Foundation for the Blind. She began touring the country to raise money for the foundation. People crowded into auditoriums to hear Helen speak. She appeared in front of state legislatures and made trips to the White House to meet with presidents. Everywhere she went, Helen worked hard to raise people's awareness of the struggles of the blind.

The American Foundation for the Blind

The American Foundation for the Blind (AFB) was established in 1921 to give people who are blind information and support. Helen Keller believed in the foundation's work and raised money by giving speeches and meeting with people all over the world. In 1946, she became the spokesperson for another organization called the American Foundation for Overseas Blind. This organization for the blind outside the United States was eventually renamed Helen Keller International. Helen continued to work for the AFB until her death in 1968.

Today, the AFB works harder than ever to help people who are blind reach their goals in life. The AFB publishes books and helps train people who teach the blind to read and to use computers. The foundation also supports people who provide job training to the blind. The AFB's goal is to help people who are blind lead productive and independent lives.

Helen traveled around the world to raise money to help people who are blind. Here, she visits with schoolchildren in Melbourne, Australia, in 1948.

Into a New Room

Helen continued her writing and lectures. In 1929, she published a book titled *Midstream: My Later Life*. After the book came out, Helen and Annie traveled to Europe with Helen's secretary, Polly Thomson. Annie's health and eyesight were failing quickly, and she wanted to see more of the world before she completely lost her sight.

After returning to the United States, Annie grew weaker. Polly took her place on fundraising trips with Helen. Between trips, Helen and Polly tried to help Annie regain her strength. But she died on October 20, 1936, at age 70. At the time of Annie's death, Helen sat at her side, holding her hand. Annie had been Helen's companion for almost 50 years.

Helen was sad about Annie's death. But she did not want to give up on her own life. In her diary, she wrote, "Life is a daring adventure or nothing." Soon Helen and Polly were off on new adventures. In 1937, they traveled to Japan and to Europe.

Polly Thomson (right) became Helen's secretary in 1914. In the 1930s, as Annie's health began to fail, Polly also became Helen's traveling companion. Helen (left), Annie (center), and Polly posed for this photograph in 1932.

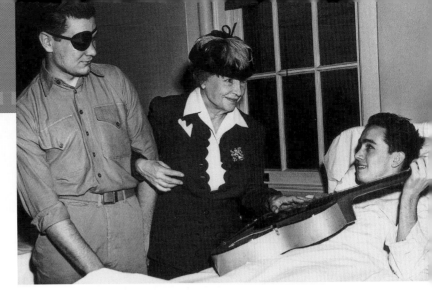

From 1943 to 1955, Helen traveled to military hospitals to visit wounded soldiers.

Helen continued to devote her life to others. During World War II (1939–1945), she made many visits to American army and navy hospitals. She talked with wounded soldiers, some of whom had lost an arm or a leg. Others had gone blind. Helen encouraged them to overcome their disabilities. She brought them hope for the future.

During the next 11 years, Helen visited 35 countries. At each visit, she spoke to crowds of supporters and raised money for people with disabilities. Helen met with government officials, urging them to set up schools for the blind and deaf. Her efforts brought new programs for people with disabilities in countries around the world.

Helen's fame grew as she became known through movies, books, plays, and TV. In 1954, a film was made about Helen's life titled *The Unconquered*. The movie was honored with an **Academy Award** in 1955. That same year, Helen finished a book about Annie Sullivan's life called *Teacher*. Two years later, a TV network showed the play *The Miracle Worker* about Helen's early life with Annie. The play also drew theater crowds in New York City. A film version of *The Miracle Worker* later won an Academy Award.

In her later years, Helen was happy to spend more time in her garden.

Helen retired from public life in 1961. She spent quiet and simple days, taking joy in walks through her garden. In 1964, Helen received a special award. President Lyndon Johnson presented Helen with the Presidential Medal of Freedom, the highest honor given to a **civilian** by the U.S. government.

Helen knew she was nearing the end of her life. On June 1, 1968, she died after a heart attack. She was 87 years old. Thousands of people attended her funeral at the National Cathedral in Washington, D.C. A special section of seats was set aside for the blind who had **seeing-eye dogs**. During the ceremony, an **interpreter** stood at the front of the church to translate the speakers' words into sign language for the deaf. After the funeral service, Helen's ashes were kept in the cathedral next to those of her teacher, Annie Sullivan.

Helen was once asked if she believed in life after death. She replied, "Most certainly. It is no more than passing from one room to another." Then Helen added, "But there's a difference for me, you know. Because in that other room I will be able to see."

> *"No one knows better than I the bitter denials of life. But I have made my limitations tools of learning and true joy."*
> —Helen Keller

Did You Know?

Dogs brought great happiness to Helen throughout her life. "I loved their affectionate ways and the eloquent wags of their tails," she wrote.

- Helen loved dogs and owned many during her lifetime. She believed dogs sensed that she was blind and deaf. They always stood when she was near so she wouldn't stumble over them.

- As a child, Helen became friends with the famous author Mark Twain and with Alexander Graham Bell, the inventor of the telephone.

- Helen enjoyed music and art. She was able to feel the vibrations of instruments, and she liked to put her hand on a singer's throat. Her favorite kind of art was **sculpture**. She ran her hands over pieces of sculpture to feel their curves and designs.

- Helen met every president of the United States who served after she turned 8 years old.

- Helen strongly believed all people deserve to be treated fairly. In addition to speaking out for the disabled, she often voiced her support for the rights of women and blacks.

- Helen's first book, *The Story of My Life*, has been published in at least 50 languages.

- *Time* magazine named Helen Keller one of the 100 most important people of the 20th century.

Helen visited with President John F. Kennedy in 1961.

Important Dates

June 27, 1880: Helen Keller is born in Tuscumbia, Alabama.

February 1882: Helen loses her sight, hearing, and ability to speak. (age 1)

March 3, 1887: Annie Sullivan becomes Helen's teacher. (age 6)

1888: Helen arrives to study at the Perkins Institution for the Blind in Boston, Massachusetts.

1900: Helen enters Radcliffe College. (age 20)

1903: Helen publishes *The Story of My Life*.

1904: Helen graduates from Radcliffe College. (age 24)

1908: Helen writes and publishes *The World I Live In*.

1914: Helen hires Polly Thomson as her secretary.

1918: Helen stars in *Deliverance*.

1924: Helen joins the American Foundation for the Blind. (age 44)

1929: Helen writes and publishes *Midstream*.

1936: Annie Sullivan dies.

1937: Helen and Polly tour Europe and Japan. (age 57)

1941: The United States enters World War II.

1943: Helen begins visits to wounded American soldiers in military hospitals.

1954: *The Unconquered*, a movie about Helen, is released.

1955: Helen publishes *Teacher*, a book about Annie Sullivan. (age 75)

1957: *The Miracle Worker* is first performed on stage.

1960: Polly Thomson dies.

1964: Helen receives the Presidential Medal of Freedom.

June 1, 1968: Helen dies at her home in Easton, Connecticut. (age 87)

Nellie Bly (1867–1922)

Nellie Bly was the pen name of Elizabeth Cochrane Seaman, a journalist known for her daring reporting. Bly once got herself arrested to find out how the police treated women prisoners. Another time, she went undercover inside a mental hospital. Her stories brought about better treatment for the mentally ill.

Rachel Carson (1907–1964)

Rachel Carson was a biologist who wrote about the ways all living things depend on one another. Her book *The Sea Around Us*, was on the bestseller list for 86 weeks. She also wrote a book called *Silent Spring*, which explored how chemicals called pesticides harm the environment. Carson's books helped people understand how pollution affects rivers, soil, and water.

Annie Oakley (1860–1926)

Annie Oakley learned how to shoot a gun when she was 8 years old. By age 21, she was performing in shows as a sharpshooter. She amazed audiences in the United States and Europe with such tricks as shooting a dime out of a person's hand. Considered one of America's greatest sharpshooters, Oakley starred in Buffalo Bill's Wild West show for more than 16 years.

Georgia O'Keeffe (1887–1986)

Georgia O'Keeffe was an artist known for painting objects from nature in bright, strong colors. Her subjects included flowers and the scenery of New Mexico. Many of her paintings are abstracts. They express the idea of an object rather than show what it actually looks like. O'Keefe is considered one of the most important American artists of her time.

Eleanor Roosevelt (1884–1962)

Eleanor Roosevelt was the First Lady of the United States from 1933 to 1945. A teacher, writer, and speaker, she was the first First Lady to have a career. She also set up programs to help Americans through the Great Depression, and she visited soldiers during World War II. In later years, Roosevelt served in the United Nations and became a champion of human rights.

Glossary

Academy Award (uh-KA-duh-mee uh-WARD) an honor given to a film or the people who worked on a film from the Academy of Motion Picture Arts and Sciences; Academy Awards, which are also called Oscars, are presented each year.

Braille (BRAYL) a reading system developed for people who are blind by Louis Braille in the 1820s; Braille uses groupings of raised dots that the blind read by feeling with their fingertips.

civilian (sih-VILL-yuhn) a person who is not a member of the armed forces

communicate (ku-MYOO-nuh-kayt) to share ideas, information, and feelings with another person

disability (dis-uh-BILL-uh-tee) a condition that limits what someone can do; people with disabilities often find different ways of doing things that help them overcome their limits.

essay (ESS-ay) a piece of writing about a certain subject

frustrate (FRUST-rayt) to feel helpless or discouraged because you are stopped again and again when you try to do something

gesture (JESS-chur) to make a movement with your head, arms, hands, or other body part to communicate a message

interpreter (in-TER-prit-er) a person who explains the meanings of words used by one person to another person; interpreters help people who do not use the same language communicate.

prejudice (PREJ-uh-diss) to judge a person or group of people without knowing the facts

sculpture (SKUHLP-chur) a piece of art carved out of stone, wood, or clay; sculptures also can be made from metal that has melted and then cooled and hardened in a mold.

seeing-eye dog (SEE-ing-EYE DAWG) a dog that has been trained to help someone who is blind or has trouble seeing

vibration (vy-BRAY-shuhn) a very fast back and forth motion; when we speak, vocal chords vibrate to make sound.

To Learn More

READ THESE BOOKS

Nonfiction

Alexander, Sally Hobart. *Do You Remember the Color Blue? And Other Questions Kids Ask about Blindness*. New York: Viking, 2000.

Bowen, Andy Russell. *A World of Knowing: A Story about Thomas Hopkins Gallaudet*. Minneapolis: Carolrhoda Books, 1995.

Flodin, Mickey. *Signing for Kids*. New York: Putnam, 1991.

Freedman, Russell. *Out of Darkness: The Story of Louis Braille*. New York: Clarion Books, 1997.

Keller, Helen. *The Story of My Life*. New York: Modern Library, 2003.

Sullivan, George. *Helen Keller*. New York: Scholastic, 2000.

Fiction

Denenberg, Barry. *Mirror, Mirror on the Wall: The Diary of Bess Brennan*. New York: Scholastic, 2002.

Matlin, Marlee. *Deaf Child Crossing*. New York: Simon & Schuster, 2002.

LOOK UP THESE INTERNET SITES

The Braille Alphabet

www.nbp.org/alph.html
View the Braille alphabet that Helen used to read, then type in your name to see it in Braille.

Helen Keller Kids Museum Online

www.afb.org/braillebug/hkmuseum.asp
Learn more about Helen's life through photographs and fun facts.

Ivy Green: Birthplace of Helen Keller

www.helenkellerbirthplace.org
Explore the home where Helen Keller grew up through photos and descriptions of the house and grounds.

Sign the Alphabet

http://www.funbrain.com/signs/index.html
Play a game that helps you learn how to sign the alphabet.

Internet search key words:

Helen Keller, Annie Sullivan, blind, deaf, manual alphabet, Braille, American Sign Languag

Index